MENTAL HEALTH RESPONSE TO MASS VIOLENCE AND TERRORISM

A FIELD GUIDE

U.S. DEPARTMENT OF HEALTH AND HUMAN SERVICES
Substance Abuse and Mental Health Services Administration
Center for Mental Health Services
www.samhsa.gov

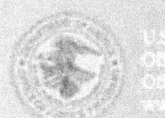

U.S. DEPARTMENT OF JUSTICE
Office of Justice Programs
Office for Victims of Crime
www.ojp.usdoj.gov/ovc

MENTAL HEALTH RESPONSE TO MASS VIOLENCE AND TERRORISM

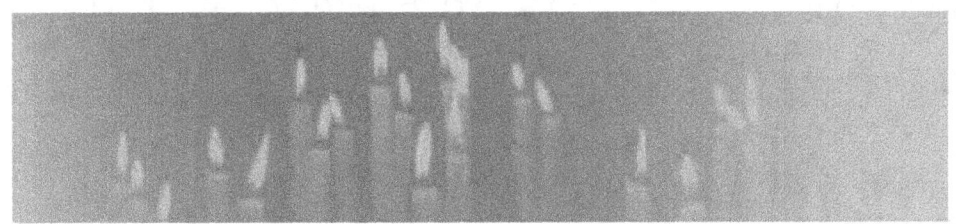

A FIELD GUIDE

U.S. Department of Health and Human Services
Substance Abuse and Mental Health Services Administration
Center for Mental Health Services
2005

ACKNOWLEDGMENTS

This publication was produced under Interagency Agree[...] #RA00C5400A between the U.S. Department of Justice ([...] Office for Victims of Crime (OVC), and the Center for Me[...] Health Services (CMHS), the Substance Abuse and Ment[...] Services Administration (SAMHSA). DOJ provided funds [...] development of the document; SAMHSA provided funds [...] editing, design, and layout of the publication; and the Fe[...] Emergency Management Agency (FEMA) provided the fu[...] printing. The document was written by Deborah J. DeWo[...] M.S.P.H., and reviewed by a group of experts on mass vio[...] and mental health response. The SAMHSA Disaster Tech[...] Assistance Center (DTAC), ESI, under contract with CMH[...] the document and designed the cover and layout for this[...] publication.

Disclaimer

The content in this publication is solely the responsibilit[...] author and does not necessarily represent the position o[...] DOJ, OVC; SAMHSA or its centers. This publication is a c[...] panion piece for *Mental Health Response to Mass Violenc[...] Terrorism: A Training Manual* (SAMHSA Publication No. S[...] 3959), and all material referenced in the *Field Guide* is cit[...] *Training Manual*, References and Additional Reading sect[...]

Public Domain Notice

Electronic Access and Copies of Publication

This publication can be accessed electronically through the following Internet connections: www.samhsa.gov and www.ncjrs.org. For additional free copies of this document, please contact SAMHSA's National Mental Health Information Center, and ask for Publication No. SMA 4025, at 1-800-789-2647, 1-866-889-2647 (TDD); or contact the OVC Resource Center, and ask for Publication No. NCJ 205452, at 1-800-851-3420, 1-877-712-9279 (TTY).

Recommended Citation

U.S. Department of Health and Human Services. *Mental Health Response to Mass Violence and Terrorism: A Field Guide.* DHHS Pub. No. SMA 4025. Rockville, MD: Center for Mental Health Services, Substance Abuse and Mental Health Services Administration, 2005.

Originating Office

Substance Abuse and Mental Health Services Administration
1 Choke Cherry Road, Rockville, Maryland 20857
DHHS Publication No. SMA 4025
Printed 2005

TABLE OF CONTENTS

INTRODUCTION

This *Field Guide* is intended for mental health and disaster workers; first responders; government agency employees; and crime victim assistance, faith-based, healthcare, and other service providers who assist survivors and families during the aftermath of mass violence and terrorism. All who come in contact with victims and families can contribute to restoring their dignity and sense of control by interacting with sensitivity, kindness, and respect. This *Field Guide* provides the basics of responding to those in crisis.

Human-caused events such as mass shootings, bombings, riots, exposure to biohazards, and acts of terrorism are deliberately planned and perpetrated for political, sociocultural, revenge-motivated, or hate-based reasons. Acts of mass violence and terrorism target a building, neighborhood, particular site, or event. Those confronted with life threat, mass casualties, overwhelming terror, and human suffering may experience severe psychological stress and trauma. Survivors, families, and the affected communities cope not only with the resulting deaths, injuries, and destruction but also with the horrific knowledge that their losses were caused by intentional human malevolence. When rescue and recovery efforts extend over weeks and months, family members endure prolonged uncertainty and an ongoing threat of possible future attacks, which contribute to heightened anxiety and a sense of vulnerability. These traumatic realities also impact first responders, media personnel, government officials, and others whose job-related responsibilities bring them in contact with the disaster's tragic impact.

Because disasters caused by mass violence and acts of terrorism are also crimes, law enforcement and the criminal justice system fill primary roles. When the underlying motivation is terrorism, Federal criminal justice agencies are responsible for the investigation and prosecution. The disaster's impact zone becomes a

secured crime scene. Crime victims and their families ha
legal right to receive information about criminal justice a
participate in the criminal justice process, and receive pr
from intimidation and harassment. They may apply for b
and compensation for crime-related expenses. This inter
emergency response, criminal justice, and disaster relief.
recovery systems is a defining feature of the response to
violence and terrorism.

This *Field Guide* includes essential information about sur
and family members' reactions and needs, with specific s
tions for assisting children, adolescents, adults, and older
It describes basic "helping" skills with indicators for whe
someone to a licensed mental health professional. The la
section presents strategies for worker* stress prevention
management.

This *Field Guide* draws from material contained in *Menta.
Response to Mass Violence and Terrorism: A Training Manu
highlights practical approaches. The *Training Manual* pro
indepth and comprehensive information, and references
additional reading.

*In this *Field Guide*, the term "worker" refers to service provider
others who assist survivors and families.

KEY PRINCIPLES FOR MENTAL HEALTH INTERVENTION

Workers assisting survivors and family members may find the following key principles helpful, as they frequently are used by seasoned crime victim assistance and disaster mental health professionals:

- No one who witnesses the consequences of mass criminal violence is unaffected by it.

- Mass violence and terrorism result in two types of human impact— individual and community.

- Mental health, crime victim assistance and other human services must be uniquely and individually tailored to the communities they serve. Cultural competence is essential.

- While most traumatic stress and grief reactions are normal responses to extraordinary circumstances, a significant minority of survivors experience serious, long-term psychological difficulties.

◆ Most survivors and families respond to active, genuine
and concern. However, some will reject services of all l

◆ Mental health assistance is practical, flexible, empowe
respectful of survivors' needs to pace their exposure to
realities resulting from the event. First and foremost, p
must **do no harm** when intervening.

◆ Procedures and protocols used by emergency services
enforcement, medical examiners' offices, and the crim
justice system can confuse and distress survivors. Clea
sensitive explanations are helpful.

◆ Support from family, friends, and the community helps
survivors and families cope with trauma and loss.

When mass violence occurs, innocent and unsuspecting
are caught by surprise in the course of their daily routine
people usually are well-functioning and resilient. They ha
capacity to cope with the profound psychological deman
losses they experience. Communities, families, and socia
systems pull together to comfort and support those most
impacted.

Workers providing emotional support take a practical, do
earth approach. They reach out to survivors and respectf
reassurance, a listening ear, a warm beverage, concrete i
tion about what will happen next, and practical assistanc
immediate tasks. Survivors and families may gather at de
sites such as community centers, schools, employment s
local places of worship, and disaster relief centers. They i
think they need "psychological counseling" or "mental he
services" but may welcome genuine concern and help to
with the stress. "Mental health support" can even take pli
a cup of coffee.

Communities vary in their cultural, racial, and ethnic con
positions including: the presence of refugee or immigran

the primary languages spoken, and demographic and socio-economic characteristics. A particular group may have been the target of violence due to prejudice or hate. If the alleged perpetrators are from a particular country or group, U.S. citizens and residents with similar physical characteristics or origins may be at risk for harassment and retaliatory violence. Crisis mental health support must help each affected group in the community.

Tailor Support to Community Needs

✔ Be culturally sensitive.

✔ Provide information and services in the appropriate language.

✔ Understand the disaster's specific impact on affected cultural groups.

✔ Collaborate and consult with trusted organizations and community leaders to serve all members of the community.

SURVIVORS' AND FAMILIES' IMMEDIATE NEEDS

Experiencing an act of terrorism or mass violence involving exposure to mass casualties, extreme trauma, and threats causes predictable human reactions. Most survivors and families have the same initial concerns and needs. They accept relief efforts more readily when first responders, emergency managers, law enforcement personnel, human services workers, and government officials consider the following:

- Physical need for warmth, safety, rest, fluids, and food.

- Emotional need for protection, comfort, control, reassurance, and a "listening ear."

- Fear and anxiety about the safety and well-being of loved ones, friends, and coworkers.

- Need for connection with loved ones and support systems.

◆ Desire for frequent updates regarding the status of res‹ recovery efforts, criminal investigations, potential thre. what is going to happen next.

◆ Need for clear, sensitive explanations of: emergency m procedures; medical examiner's office procedures and protocols; the criminal justice process; the rationale fo impact operational decisions; and immediately availab services, benefits, grants, and assistance.

◆ Need for death notification conducted in a straightforv clear, and compassionate manner.

◆ Normal trauma reactions such as fearfulness, numbne jumpiness, sleep and concentration problems, and rep traumatic images and sounds.

In the days and weeks following mass violent victimizati shock gives way to the realization of personal losses. Th‹ changing implications of death, the destruction of home community, serious injuries, and the loss of a sense of sa security in the world become increasingly apparent. Othe quences such as loss of employment, and relocation of h school, or place of worship exacerbate disruption and gr‹ Survivors and families psychologically pace themselves ‹ to individual timeframes and personal coping styles.

Survivors and families often face numerous logistical an‹ practical issues that can seem overwhelming. Workers m facilitate assistance with transportation, child care, locati missing loved one or pet, funeral arrangements, finding temporary housing, filling prescriptions, replacing eyegla and providing healthy foods and beverages. They also m‹ facilitate filling out the necessary paperwork for obtainin victim compensation and benefits, a death certificate, di‹ related unemployment, insurance benefits, and financial assistance. Through helping with practical tasks, worker‹ earn survivors' trust and the privilege to support them w express their pain, fear, sorrow, and anger.

PSYCHOLOGICAL FIRST AID AND COUNSELING SKILLS

Workers should approach survivors and family members with compassion and regard for their humanity and dignity. This includes honoring families' and survivors' wishes to be left alone or deal privately with their suffering. Workers enhance survivors' sense of control over their situation through recognizing and reinforcing their coping strengths, providing clear information, and offering choices when appropriate. When survivors feel more secure and in control, they can better address immediate challenges. Crisis support involves guiding, listening, reassuring, and providing practical assistance. The following section provides "nuts-and-bolts" suggestions.

Establishing Rapport

When making initial contact, workers should introduce t]
selves and briefly explain their roles. They may ask perm
sit down, since standing over people when they are seate
seem intimidating. Workers convey genuine interest and
through eye contact, the assurance of safety, offering a w
beverage, and a calm presence. They provide comfort, su
and nonjudgmental response to expressed immediate ne
Trust and safety are enhanced when workers listen to wl
distressed survivors and family members choose to discu
avoid asking intrusive questions.

Active Listening

Workers listen most effectively when they absorb informa
through their ears, eyes, and hearts. Some tips for effectiv
listening are:

◆ **Support personal "pacing"**—Many survivors and far
members want to talk about their traumatic experienc
Putting terrifying and tragic experiences into words ar
them heard while receiving emotional support can col
to the healing process. Others may choose to focus on
tasks or seemingly inconsequential matters, temporar:
avoiding direct discussion of their trauma and loss. W(
should look for cues regarding comfort levels, coping s
appropriate pacing, and allow survivors and family me
take the lead with personal sharing.

◆ **Allow silence**—Silence can give a person time to refle
become aware of feelings. Silence may help survivors :
what is most important to them at the moment, or be
for elaboration on thoughts and reactions. Simply "bei
the survivor or family member can be supportive.

◆ **Attend nonverbally**—Eye contact, head nodding, cari
expressions, and being at the same physical level (e.g.,

standing) let the person know that the worker is listening. Observing and heeding cultural differences with regard to non-verbal communication conveys cultural sensitivity and can enhance acceptance of help.

♦ **Paraphrase**—The worker conveys understanding, interest, and empathy by repeating portions of what the person has said. Paraphrasing also checks for accuracy, clarifies misunderstandings, and lets the person know that he or she is being heard. Good lead-ins are: "So you are saying that...," "It sounds like you...," or "I have heard you say that...." Paraphrasing may seem awkward at first, but is an effective tool for building trust.

♦ **Reflect feelings**—The worker may notice that the person's tone of voice or nonverbal gestures suggest emotions such as anger, sadness, or fear. Possible responses are, "You seem afraid of spending the night at home alone. Is that true?" This helps the person to identify and articulate emotions and needs.

♦ **Allow expression of emotions**—Communicating intense emotions through tears or venting is an important part of healing. It often helps the survivor or family member work through feelings so that he/she can better address the immediate tasks at hand. Workers should stay relaxed and let the person know that it is okay to feel and express emotions. [Suggestions in the "Stress Prevention, Management, and Intervention" section may be helpful.]

Some Possible Do's and Definite Don'ts

Do say:

✔ You have temporarily lost your sense of safety and security. You will feel better over time.

✔ It is understandable that you feel this way.

✔ This is your body's and mind's way of dealing with wł happened to you. Your reactions are normal.

✔ Feeling intense emotions and having thoughts that yc never had before is normal. You are not going crazy.

✔ You didn't do anything wrong. It wasn't your fault. You best you could.

✔ Things will never be the same as they were, but you w gradually feel better.

Don't say:

✔ It could have been worse. You're lucky that....

✔ It's best if you just stay busy.

✔ You should count your blessings, it will make you feel

✔ I know just how you feel.

✔ He/she is in a better place now.

✔ You need to get on with your life.

While the human desire is to try to "fix" the survivor's or member's painful situation or to make them feel better, h comments in the preceding "Don't Say," however, can mɛ person feel discounted, judged, misunderstood, or more ɛ Workers may find it difficult not to overidentify with surv families. They should allow survivors and families the spɛ their own experiences, feelings, and perspectives—whate are. Simply listening with respect, concern, and calmnes: comfort them.

Psychological First Aid

During and immediately after an act of mass violence or terrorism, those most affected may experience shock, confusion, fear, numbness, panic, and anxiety. They may "shut down."

Witnessing or suspecting the death of loved ones or friends can be emotionally overwhelming. Some people may be locked in disbelief. When the perpetrators have not been apprehended or the event is considered terrorism, all may experience a sense of continued threat and danger. Workers have seven immediate tasks and purposes:

1. Identify those in need of medical attention for intense stress reactions.

2. Provide protection from further harm, and assistance to a safe environment.

3. Ensure that survivors are warm/cool enough and are being given fluids and food.

4. Promote a sense of security through orienting and reassurance.

5. Connect survivors with family, friends, and loved ones.

6. Provide information about the crime scene and perpetrators, status of rescue efforts, and what will happen next.

7. Connect survivors and family members with resources for immediate help (e.g., voluntary agencies, crime victim assistance, systems for locating missing persons, emergency shelter and food, faith-based resources, and disaster mental health and psychiatry).

Problem Solving

Stress resulting from trauma, crime victimization, and su bereavement often causes disorganized thinking, concer problems, and difficulty planning and making decisions. people react by feeling overwhelmed and may become ei immobilized or unproductively overactive. Workers can encourage survivors and family members to participate i concrete tasks to help them focus and assume a more ac in coping. Also, workers can guide individuals through th following problem-solving steps to help prioritize and ad immediate issues.

◆ **Identify current priority needs and problems anc possible solutions**

"Describe the problems/challenges that you are facing ri

Selecting one solvable problem and then successfully addressing it can help restore a sense of control and c Avoid picking a complex problem first. Support the pei identifying a task that is easily completed.

◆ **Assess functioning and coping**

"How are you doing? How do you feel about how you ar coping?"

"How have you handled stressful life events in the past?"

Through observation, gently asking questions, and rev the magnitude of the person's problems and loss, the i develops an impression of the person's capacity to ad current challenges. Based on this assessment, the wor point out coping strengths, facilitate the person's engagement with social supports, or make referrals. The worker may also seek consultation from a medical or mental health professional.

◆ Evaluate available resources

"Who might be able to help you with this task/problem?"

"What resources and options might be helpful?"

Explore existing sources of assistance and support such as immediate and extended family, loved ones, friends, neighbors, coworkers, religious leaders, and healthcare providers. Connect the survivor or family member with the appropriate community, crime victim assistance, and disaster relief resources and assess if he/she is able to make the calls and complete the required paperwork. Assist with accessing resources when necessary.

◆ Develop and implement a plan

"What steps will you take to address this problem?"

Encourage the survivor or family member to say out loud what they plan to do and how. Offer to check in for support and to see how he/she is doing. If the worker has agreed to perform a task or get information, it is very important to follow through. A plan may focus on a very short timeframe or limited actions. For example, a plan could be to make two phone calls. Being reliable and following up, even when there is no new information, helps survivors gain control. Workers should promise only what they can do, not what they **would like** to do.

A Word of Caution

When confronted with a survivor's or family member's se overwhelming and heart-wrenching needs, workers can understandable impulse to help in every way possible. W may become over-involved and do too much for the surv grieving family, which is usually not in the survivor's or fa best interest. While being helpful and available, workers s also convey their confidence in the individual's coping ak and resilience. When survivors and families are empowei address their own problems, they feel more capable to ta next challenge.

Confidentiality

The privilege of helping others carries ethical responsibil Helping people in need involves learning their problems, concerns, fears, and anxieties—sometimes with very pers details. This sharing must be done with a sense of trust, I upon mutual respect, and the understanding that all disc are confidential. No person's situation or "case" should b discussed elsewhere without the consent of the person b helped, except in extreme situations when the worker be person might harm him/herself or others. Under those ci stances, workers should report concerns to their supervis that the appropriate authorities may be contacted.

Workers should avoid discussing information in public pl such as restaurants, that might give the impression that p not being protected. Only by maintaining the trust and re the survivor or family member can the privilege of helpin continue.

WHEN TO REFER FOR MENTAL HEALTH SERVICES

Workers should make referrals to mental health and other healthcare professionals when they encounter survivors and family members with severe physical or emotional reactions. Some may have preexisting physical or psychiatric conditions that have worsened because of traumatic stress. The following reactions, behaviors, and symptoms signal a need for the worker to consult with his or her supervisor and, in most cases, refer the person for assessment and more specialized assistance. In all instances, **when in doubt, consult.**

♦ *Disorientation:* The person is dazed and unable to give date or time, location, and events of the past 24 hours, or understand what is happening.

♦ *Anxiety and Hyperarousal:* The person is highly agitated, restless, jumpy, and on edge; is unable to sleep; has frequent disturbing

nightmares, flashbacks, and intrusive thoughts; or broo
circumstances surrounding the event.

◆ **Dissociation:** The person exhibits pronounced emotio
disconnection, an incomplete awareness of the trauma
experience, a sense of seeing him/herself from another
perspective, a perception that the environment is unre
time is distorted.

◆ **Depression:** The person exhibits pervasive feelings of
hopelessness and despair; unshakeable feelings of wor
lessness, guilt, or self-blame; frequent crying for no ap
reason; withdrawal from others; or inability to engage
productive activity.

◆ **Mental Illness:** Symptoms include hearing voices, see
things or people that are not there, delusional thinking
appearing out of touch with reality, and excessive pre-
occupation with an idea or thought.

◆ **Inability to Care for Self:** The person does not eat, ba
change clothes; is apathetic, isolated from others, and
to manage activities of daily living.

◆ **Suicidal or Homicidal Thoughts or Plans:** The pers
makes statements like "I can't go on," "I just want to e
terrible pain I'm feeling," "I wish that I had died," "I wa
my husband in heaven," or "I'm going to get even." Th
feels pervasive self-blame or sense of responsibility for
person's death.

◆ **Problematic Use of Alcohol or Drugs:** The person n
references to getting drunk, getting high, or not being
stop drinking; blocks out pain with mood-altering subs
relapses from previous abstinence; misses work or oth
obligations due to alcohol or drug use; or expresses co
about a family member's substance use.

◆ **Domestic Violence, Child Abuse, or Elder Abuse:** T
person mentions instances of inappropriate anger or v
toward family members.

POPULATIONS WITH SPECIAL NEEDS

Terrorism and mass violence inevitably touch all who are in their zone of impact. This zone may include people of different ages and economic means; people of various cultural, racial, and ethnic backgrounds; people with different sexual orientations and family configurations; people who speak foreign languages; people from many occupational groups; and people who have roles in emergency response and recovery efforts.

The basic human need for survival, safety, protection, connection with loved ones, and accurate information are shared, while additional needs may be more specific to a particular group. Workers are most effective when they are informed about, respectful of, and responsive to the various groups in the affected community. Special consideration should be given to the following groups as well as others with special needs:

◆ Age groups (e.g., children, teenagers, older adults);

◆ Highly impacted survivors and families;

◆ Cultural, ethnic, and racial groups;

◆ People with serious and persistent mental illness;

◆ Human service, criminal justice, and emergency respo
workers.

Age Groups

Each age group is vulnerable in unique ways to the stress
trauma, victimization, and sudden bereavement. Some o
reactions listed in Table 1 may be immediate, while othei
appear months later. Table 1 describes possible behavior
physical, and emotional reactions of different age groups
options for helpful intervention.

TABLE 1:	REACTIONS TO TRAUMA AND SUGGESTIONS FOR INTERVENTION			
Ages	Behavioral	Physical	Emotional	Intervention Options
1-5	• Clinging to parents or familiar adults • Helplessness and passive behavior • Resumption of bed wetting or thumb sucking • Fear of the dark • Avoidance of sleeping alone • Increased crying	• Loss of appetite • Stomach aches • Nausea • Sleep problems, nightmares • Speech difficulties • Tics	• Anxiety • Generalized fear • Irritability • Angry outbursts • Sadness • Withdrawal	• Give verbal reassurance and physical comfort • Clarify misconceptions repeatedly • Provide comforting bedtime routines • Help with labels for emotions • Avoid unnecessary separations • Permit child to sleep in parents' room temporarily • Demystify reminders • Encourage expression regarding losses (deaths, pets, toys) • Monitor media exposure • Encourage expression through play activities

Continued on next page

TABLE 1:	REACTIONS TO TRAUMA AND SUGGESTIONS FOR INTERVENTION			
Ages	Behavioral	Physical	Emotional	Interventi
6-11	• Decline in school performance • School avoidance • Aggressive behavior at home or school • Hyperactive or silly behavior • Whining, clinging, acting like a younger child • Increased competition with younger siblings for parents' attention • Traumatic play and reenactments	• Change in appetite • Headaches • Stomach aches • Sleep disturbances, nightmares • Somatic complaints	• Fear of feelings • Withdrawal from friends, familiar activities • Reminders triggering fears • Angry outbursts • Preoccupation with crime, criminals, safety, and death • Self-blame • Guilt	• Give add attention considera • Relax exp performa and at sc temporar • Set gentl limits for behavior • Provide s but unde home ch rehabilita activities • Encouraç and play of though feelings • Listen to repeated traumatic • Clarify ch distortion misconce • Identify a with remi • Develop program support, activities, on traum prepared planning, at-risk ch

TABLE 1:	REACTIONS TO TRAUMA AND SUGGESTIONS FOR INTERVENTION			
Ages	Behavioral	Physical	Emotional	Intervention Options
12-18	• Decline in academic performance • Rebellion at home or school • Decline in previous responsible behavior • Agitation or decrease in energy level, apathy • Delinquent behavior • Risk-taking behavior • Social withdrawal • Abrupt shift in relationships • Use of alcohol or illegal drugs	• Appetite changes • Headaches • Gastrointestinal problems • Skin eruptions • Complaints of vague aches and pains • Sleep disorders	• Loss of interest in peer social activities, hobbies, recreation • Sadness or depression • Anxiety and fearfulness about safety • Resistance to authority • Feelings of inadequacy and helplessness • Guilt, self-blame, shame and self-consciousness • Desire for revenge	• Give additional attention and consideration • Relax expectations of performance at home and school temporarily • Encourage discussion of experience of trauma with peers, significant adults • Avoid insistence on discussion of feelings with parents • Address impulse to recklessness • Link behavior and feelings to event • Encourage physical activities • Encourage resumption of social activities, athletics, clubs, etc. • Encourage participation in community activities and school events • Develop school programs for peer support and debriefing, at-risk student support groups, telephone hotlines, drop-in centers, and identification of at-risk teens

Continued on next page

| TABLE 1: | REACTIONS TO TRAUMA AND SUGGESTIONS FOR INTERVENTION | | | |

Ages	Behavioral	Physical	Emotional	Interven
Adults	• Sleep problems • Avoidance of reminders • Excessive activity level • Protectiveness toward loved ones • Crying easily • Angry outbursts • Increased conflicts with family • Hypervigilance • Isolation, withdrawal, shutting down • Increased use of alcohol or illegal drugs	• Nausea • Headaches • Fatigue, exhaustion • Gastrointestinal distress • Appetite change • Somatic complaints • Worsening of chronic conditions	• Shock, disorientation, and numbness • Depression, sadness • Grief • Irritability, anger • Anxiety, fear • Despair, hopelessness • Guilt, self-doubt • Mood swings	• Protect, connect • Ensure emerger services • Provide listening opportur about ex losses • Provide rescue a updates resource question • Assist w and prot • Assist fa facilitate cation a functioni • Provide on traum and copi reaction: families • Provide on crimi procedu primary groups • Provide services • Assess when inc • Provide on refer

TABLE 1:	REACTIONS TO TRAUMA AND SUGGESTIONS FOR INTERVENTION			
Ages	Behavioral	Physical	Emotional	Intervention Options
Older Adults	• Withdrawal and isolation • Reluctance to leave home • Mobility limitations • Relocation adjustment problems	• Worsening of chronic illnesses • Sleep disorders • Memory problems • Somatic symptoms • Increased susceptibility to hypo and hyperthermia • Physical and sensory limitations (sight, hearing) interfere with recovery	• Depression • Despair about losses • Apathy • Confusion, disorientation • Suspicion • Agitation, anger • Fears of institution-alization • Anxiety with unfamiliar surroundings • Embarrassment about receiving "handouts"	• Provide strong and persistent verbal reassurance • Provide orienting information • Ensure physical needs are addressed (water, food, warmth) • Use multiple assessment methods as problems may be underreported • Assist with reconnecting with family and support systems • Assist in obtaining medical and financial assistance • Encourage discussion of traumatic experience, losses, and expression of emotions • Provide crime victim assistance

Highly Impacted Survivors and Families

Research has shown that those who directly experience victimization and mass traumatization, witness the seric and physical mutilation of others, or suffer the murder of one have a likelihood of intense and prolonged emotiona ioral, and physical reactions. They are likely to suffer high distress during the immediate response phase and may I ods of difficulty for years to come. Critical events that occ throughout the criminal justice process, such as trials, se hearings, and appeals, are especially significant to this gr are often linked to restimulation of psychological wound

Workers support these survivors and family members by ing respectful and practical assistance, making needed ir tion reliably available, and supporting the multiple pathw coming to terms with overwhelming trauma and loss. Re and cultural traditions; spiritual practices; community, fa personal rituals; and symbolic gestures can soothe surviv anguish and assist them with finding meaning and the c continue living. At different points during the process of to terms with loss and trauma, activities and interventior as counseling, support groups, medication, spiritual guid social activism, helping others, artistic expression, and s healing rituals may be helpful.

Cultural, Ethnic, and Racial Groups

Workers must respond sensitively and specifically to the cultural groups affected by mass violence. The death of a one, community trauma, and mass victimization are inte with cultural overlays. Rituals surrounding death, the app handling of physical remains, funerals, burials, memorial belief in an afterlife are all deeply embedded in culture ar gion. The serious injury of a family member brings famili different cultures into contact with Western medicine an healthcare delivery system. The situation may be even more challenging when English is not the family's primary language.

Cultural and ethnic groups with histories of violent oppression, terrorism, or war in their countries of origin may interpret community violence in the United States through their experiences of prior traumatization. Those who have suffered from political oppression and abuses of military power may find the prominent visibility of uniformed personnel highly distressing or even traumatizing. Some survivor groups may live in a context of poverty, discrimination, or marginalization and face high rates of violent crime in their neighborhoods, potentially making them more vulnerable to disaster impact.

Workers convey cultural sensitivity when they provide informational briefings, notifications, and applications for services and benefits in primary spoken languages. Workers must learn about each affected group's cultural norms, practices, and traditions; views regarding mental health, trauma, and grieving; and the group's local history and community politics. Establishing working relationships with trusted organizations, service providers, and community leaders often facilitates increased acceptance.

Workers communicate cultural sensitivity when they:

✔ Use culturally accepted courteous behavior (e.g., greetings, physical space, know who is considered "family");

✔ Describe their role in culturally relevant terms;

✔ Take time to establish rapport;

✔ Provide information and services in appropriate languages;

✔ Ask about cultural practices when they are unsure;

✔ Value diversity and respect differences;

✔ Develop and adapt approaches and services to fit special group needs.

People with Serious and Persistent Mental Ill

Many survivors with mental illness function fairly well fol community disaster, especially if essential services and s networks have not been interrupted. Most have the same as the general population to "rise to the occasion" and po heroically during the immediate response period. Howeve who are directly involved and traumatized by the event n additional mental health support services, medications, c talization to regain stability. For survivors previously diag with posttraumatic stress disorder (PTSD), emergency re: stimuli (e.g., sirens, helicopters, mass casualties) may trig exacerbation due to associations with prior traumatic ev

The range of support services designed for the general po is equally beneficial for survivors and family members wi mental illness. As with all special population groups, wor need to be aware of how people with mental illness perco aster assistance and services, and build bridges that facil access.

Human Service, Criminal Justice, and Emergency Response Workers

Workers in all aspects of emergency response and disast experience considerable demands to meet the needs of s families, and the community. Depending on their role, wo may be exposed to human suffering, fatalities, people wit physical injuries, family demands and anguish, communi and other difficulties. They may experience physical stres symptoms or show signs of stress overload. Indicators in irritability, over-involvement with and inability to leave th operation, difficulty focusing, being unproductive, feeling depressed, or feeling emotionally overwhelmed. Workers intervene by suggesting or using the strategies described next section.

STRESS PREVENTION, MANAGEMENT, AND INTERVENTION

Workers must cope with a range of challenging stressors. The devastating losses, casualties, destruction of property, and emotional pain of survivors and bereaved loved ones touch providers in powerful and personal ways. The emergency response working environment often involves physical hardship, unclear roles and responsibilities, limited resources, rapidly changing priorities, intrusive media attention, and long work hours.

Despite the inevitable stress associated with community crisis response, workers experience personal gratification using their skills to assist fellow humans in need. Active engagement in the disaster response can be an antidote to feelings of vulnerability, powerlessness, and outrage commonly experienced by the community.

A proactive stress management plan focuses on two cri
contexts: the organizational and the individual. Adoptin
preventive approach allows managers and workers to ar
stressors and manage potential crises rather than simpl
to them after they occur.

When stress prevention and management strategies are
operations and the organizational culture, providers fee
and supported as they engage in this emotionally dema
work. Suggestions for organizational stress prevention,
ment, and intervention are presented in Table 2, and su
for individual stress prevention, management, and inter
are presented in Table 3.

TABLE 2:	ORGANIZATIONAL APPROACHES FOR STRESS PREVENTION, MANAGEMENT, AND INTERVENTION
Dimension	**Intervention**
Effective Management Structure and Leadership	• Clear chain of command and reporting relationships • Available and accessible leads and clinical supervisors • Use of managers experienced in emergency response and community trauma
Clear Purpose, Goals, and Training	• Clearly defined intervention goals and strategies appropriate to different assignment settings (e.g., crisis intervention, community memorial) • Training and orientation for all workers
Functionally Defined Roles	• Staff who are oriented and trained according to written role descriptions for each assignment setting • When setting is under jurisdiction of another agency (e.g., Mayor's Office, Medical Examiner's Office, American Red Cross), staff are informed of mental health provider's role, contact people, and mutual expectations
Administrative Controls	• Shifts no longer than 12 hours with 12 hours off • Rotation between high, mid, and low-stress tasks • Breaks and time away from the assignment • Necessary supplies (e.g., paper, forms, pens, educational materials) • Communication tools (e.g., mobile phones, radios) • Delegating "regular" workload so workers do not attempt disaster response and usual job
Team Support	• Buddy system for support and monitoring stress reactions • Positive atmosphere of support, mutual respect, and tolerance • Clinical support, consultation, and supervision processes built on trust, safety and respect
Plan for Stress Management	• Attention to workers' functioning and stress management • "Floating through" work areas to observe signs of stress • Education about signs and symptoms of worker stress and coping strategies • Intervention plan incorporating elements from Table 3 • Exit plan for workers leaving the operation

Dimension	Intervention
Management of Workload	• Setting task priority levels with realistic work plans • Recognizing that "not having enough to do" or "waiting" is an ex[disaster mental health response
Balanced Lifestyle	• Eating nutritious food and staying hydrated, avoiding excessive (alcohol, and tobacco • Getting adequate sleep and rest, especially on longer assignmer • Getting physical exercise when possible • Maintaining contact and connection with primary social supports
Stress Reduction Strategies	• Reducing physical tension by using familiar personal strategies (deep breaths, gentle stretching, meditation, washing face and ha progressive relaxation) • Pacing self between low and high-stress activities • Using time off to "decompress" and "recharge batteries" (e.g., ge meal, watching TV, exercising, reading a novel, listening to musi bath, talking to family) • Talking about emotions and reactions with coworkers during app
Self-Awareness	• Recognizing and heeding early warning signs for stress reaction • Accepting that one may not be able to self-assess problematic s reactions • Recognizing that over-identification with or feeling overwhelmed and families' grief and trauma may signal a need for support and • Understanding the differences between professional helping rela friendships to help maintain appropriate roles and boundaries • Examining personal prejudices and cultural stereotypes • Recognizing when one's own experience with trauma or one's p(interfere with effectiveness • Being aware of personal vulnerabilities and emotional reactions ¡ importance of team and supervisor support

TABLE 3: INDIVIDUAL APPROACHES FOR STRESS PREVENTION, MANAGEMENT, AND INTER\

INTERNET SITES

American Academy of Child and Adolescent Psychiatry
http://www.aacap.org

American Psychiatric Association
http://www.psych.org

American Psychological Association
http://www.apa.org

American Red Cross
http://www.redcross.org

Federal Emergency Management Agency
http://www.fema.gov

International Society for Traumatic Stress Studies
http://www.istss.org

Mothers Against Drunk Drivers (MADD)
http://www.madd.org

**National Center for Post-Traumatic Stress Disorder/
  U.S. Department of Veteran Affairs**
http://www.ncptsd.org

National Child Traumatic Stress Network
http://www.nctsnet.org

Office for Victims of Crime/U.S. Department of Justice
http://www.ojp.usdoj.gov/ovc/

Office for Victims of Crime Resource Center
http://www.ncjrs.org

**Substance Abuse and Mental Health Services
  Administration**
http://www.samhsa.gov

U.S. Department of Health and Human Services
Substance Abuse and Mental Health Services
    Administration
Center for Mental Health Services
1 Choke Cherry Road
Rockville, MD 20857
DHHS Publication No. SMA 4025
Printed 2005

U.S. Department of Justice
Office of Justice Programs
Office for Victims of Crime
810 Seventh St., NW
Washington, DC 20531
DOJ Publication No. NCJ 205452